THE ART EXPERIENCE

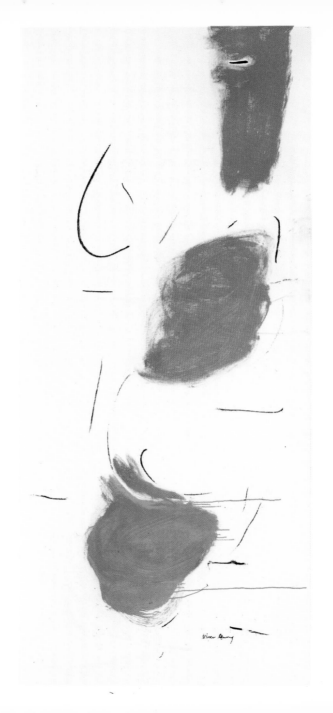

THE ART EXPERIENCE

by

VICCI SPERRY

ANDRÉ SAURET, ÉDITEUR

HENNESSEY & INGALLS, INC.
10814 WEST PICO BOULEVARD
LOS ANGELES, CALIFORNIA 90064

Library of congress catalog card number 68-26914

PRINTED IN FRANCE

CONTENTS

PART ONE

Preface 11

Chapter No.   *Page No.*

I   *ART*

      Definition 15

      Principles in Art 16

      Great Art 18

      Past and Present Art 19

II   *THE INDIVIDUAL IN ART*

      Universality 20

      Beauty 21

      Recognizing Your Own Gift 22

      Loving and Giving 23

III   *OUR RELATIONSHIP TO ORDER*

      Inspiration 24

      Harmony, Feeling 24

      Thinking and Vision, Seeing 25

      Order 26

IV   *THE PREPARATION THAT SUSTAINS*

      Tools 28

      Preparation 28

      Discipline 29

      Intuition 30

Chapter No.			Page No.
V	DRAWING		
	Purpose	32
	Line – Outline	33
VI	PAINTING		
	Freedom	34
	Light	35
	Color	36
	Life Forces	38
VII	CONTENT OF ART		
	Space	41
	Form	43
	Objects	43
	The Figure	44
VIII	GROWTH		
	Experience	46
	Expression	47
	The Journey to the Universal	48

PART TWO

Approach No.		Page No.
I	Charcoal	53
II	Mountains	54
III	Still Life – Objects in Space	55
IV	How the Individual Sees the Figure	56
V	The All-Inclusive Figure	57
VI	In the Park	58
VII	Tempera	59
VIII	Three Oranges on Different Planes	61
IX	Tropical Invitation	62
X	Drama on a Beach	63
XI	Light on Dark, Dark on Light	64
XII	Still Life – Infinite Relationships	65
XIII	Shapes of Lakes	66
XIV	More Shapes – More Lakes	67

Approach No.		Page No.
XV	Still Life – Painting Space	68
XVI	Space Relationships – Animals on a Hill . . .	69
XVII	Complete World with One Element	70
XVIII	Oil Paint	71
XIX	Still Life – Forces, Same as in Landscapes . .	72
XX	Color as Light – Three Colors	74
XXI	Three Colors on One Plane	76
XXII	Still Life – Space Not a Backdrop	77
XXIII	Four Colors on One Plane – Not Touching . .	78
XXIV	Four Colors – To Edge of Canvas	79
XXV	Four Colors Touching One Another	80
XXVI	Continuity of One Plane Using Eight or More Colors	82
XXVII	Light as Color – Still Life	84
XXVIII	Trees	86
XXIX	Figure Related to Still Life	87
XXX	Introducing Black as a Color	88
XXXI	Utilizing the World Around You	89
XXXII	Great Movements – Large Masses	90
XXXIII	Stars – Space Is Alive – Infinity	92

LIST OF PLATES

1 - AUGUST
Oil (1968) . . . . opposite title page

2 - CHILD WITH RED FACE
Oil (1966) . . . . opposite chapter 3 "Our relationship to order"

3 - TWO FIGURES WITH FALLING LEAVES
Oil (1966) . . . . opposite chapter 6 "Painting"

4 - FROM THE EARTH
Oil (1967) . . . . opposite chapter 8 "Growth"

PREFACE

THIS is a radical book—it is radical because, in a world that dwells on horror and frustration, it is an affirmation of beauty and man's high potential. The power of beauty is revealed in the words of the great Russian astronaut, Leonov, the first man who stepped out into space: "How bright it is—how incredibly beautiful!" When he was asked if he had been afraid, he replied that he was so enthralled by the radiant beauty of color that there was no place for any other feelings—that it was so "incredibly beautiful" he forgot to be afraid.

The aim of this book is to stir the thinking to a new base so that stereotyped vision yields to the newness of inspiration—and thus releases the energies of expression.

All the ideas in this book emanate from my own work as an artist and from my teaching and lecturing experience. Knowing how these ideas have helped and given inspiration to innumerable people, I would have felt most selfish if I had not labored to send them forth.

The approaches are original and inspired by the need of the artist, the teacher, and the student to acquire greater depths of understanding. Although the approaches are directed to the painter, this book goes beyond painting to the realm of all creative endeavor. It is for all who seek the development of innate abilities and talent.

Vicci SPERRY

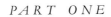

PART ONE

CHAPTER ONE

ART

DEFINITION. Art is the joyous and spontaneous evidence of man's capacity to express his deep feelings for beauty, order, life, and love. The more we know about the true nature of art, the more we know about our own abilities and feelings.

A work of art is an expression of a complete idea. It reflects the conscious and unconscious thinking of the artist. Art does not come off a production line and cannot be the product of a machine. The shallow novelty often has quick acceptance, and the profound idea usually moves slowly.

Cezanne talked of the necessity of feeling life and warmth with every step in an art experience. True art is never cold, lifeless, pulseless, or stereotyped. In Cezanne's paintings the planes unite with tenderness and every part is related to the whole. Everything in a great work of art supports everything else with a resultant sense of glory. It is inspired by the thought "I want to give something. I want to make this beautiful."

Poor painting keeps us low on the earth. Good painting, like good music, liberates.

There is no work of art with form alone, space must be in the consciousness. A great work of art no matter how complex moves on one great plane— a poor work of art has areas that do not bring us back to the aliveness of the one great plane. This great plane in painting is not flat like that of design, but has a breathing, living depth.

Art does not repeat itself. It breathes a life that imparts a newness of being. No part of good painting is superfluous or extraneous. Everything in the work of art is a breathing part of the whole. There must be a continuity of flow which includes the smallest detail.

Lesser artists add embellishments. If there is ornament it cannot become more obtrusive than the whole. It should be like a breeze that belongs to the total atmosphere. A work of art, in its completeness, is the all-inclusiveness of an expansive idea.

It is your own work and your devotion of thought that makes the ideas come. Only that which is truly real can become authentic for you.

A great painting reflects the lyrical rhythm of the infinity of nature. Your painting reflects the individuality that is maintained in nature. Bach, Mozart, Rembrandt, Cezanne, and others knew when they were in harmony with that which makes the spirit soar, with that which lifts man high above the daily wear and tear of human existence. Persistently and patiently they worked on the principles and exercises so necessary to the growth of their expression. Their greatest work has an eternal quality, a rhythm and a drama that resolves into a sublime equipoise. Cezanne was a poet in paint who felt the lyrical relationship between form and space, space and form. The glory of space was always uppermost in his consciousness. Within this space were infinite planes and relationships—everything coming under one great continuity. He translated everything into a reflection of the infinity of nature.

PRINCIPLES IN ART

Contemplation. All art comes from contemplation. Art always has existed and always will. The nature of art is all-inclusive, not decisive. It is inspiring and makes one feel harmonious and included. Art is based on intuition and is involved with organization, depth of space, and continuity. It is forever living and expanding. Intuition is its source and wellspring. Intuition is our guide. Intuition is our native endowment, our primitive intelligence. True intuition is never wrong, it makes our decisions for us. The so-called art that relies on vogue and innovation, the catering to fashion—new or old—violates the newness and the aliveness of intuition and cannot endure. Intuition unites with contemplation.

Organization. Organization in art reflects the universal law of oneness within which everything is related. Within this oneness the forms and the space unite on the rhythm of the movement. More and more, we allow ourselves to feel the depth of space. A painting moves out into universal space and at the same time is completely contained. A true work of art is all-embracing and is never detached from humanity. These qualities motivate the organization which is always alive and never inert.

Dynamics. That which is alive expresses itself in dynamics. Art cannot be contained within a finite, static pattern. Art, being the reflection of life, is a force which is the reverse of the static. The great rhythms that we see out of doors—the endless sky, the horizon, the vertical of the tree, the horizontal of the lake, the inhalation and exhalation of breathing, the ebb and flow of the tide—all are related to the living dynamics of art.

Love. Love of nature, of man, and of beauty are primary forces that desire expression. The love of color, life, form spurs the devotion and activity needed for the concentrated effort. There is much that is cold and lifeless that poses as art, but the great works of Bach, Shakespeare, and Rembrandt ennoble us and make us feel more loving.

Art is a state of caring—there is no place for indifference. Caring for someone always takes deep feeling. Caring for beauty and for mankind is the motive power for the art expression. It is a sharing. Profound music, poetry, and art inspire us with compassion, joy, and love.

Joy. The joy we bring to our work releases our capacities. There is no formula in art. We cannot say that it must be in a certain way. A great artist hardly needs to sign his name. We recognize his individuality through his work.

Art rises above the temporal into that which is lasting. What are the elements of art?—The elements of true art are light, space, and form. Objects, relationships, and qualities become alive and significant when carried on the expansiveness of joyous creativity. Joy brings freedom.

Art is truly an expression of one's own individuality and is created without dependence on another. The depth of art is a universal language that speaks to the universal quality in man.

GREAT ART. Emerson said that every genuine work of art has as much reason for being as the earth and the sun. Our concern is with art in its highest form. We may respect the skill of commercial art, but we recognize the difference of motivation. That which is called fine art evolves from the highest originality and expresses timeless individual freedom. Great art, although it includes technique, transcends technique. Its spiritual qualities are its reality.

We seem to live in a promotional world. The new is sometimes merely sensational and temporal and has little foundation Much of what is called art is motivated by what will sell at the moment. The great individuals of all times enrich our lives. The artists that are lost in a vogue are eventually forgotten. This so-called art may have temporary popularity, but does not possess the depth of feeling and the originality of true art. Great art has been achieved by the utmost dedication and courage. The contribution of great art is the sublime nourishment passed on from generation to generation.

We reflect life and, therefore, our art reflects life. Art is not an escape. It is a conviction. If there is not truthfulness, there is not great art. Because art reflects life, art is never static. Just as in music, there is in painting a continuous flow of rhythm that reflects the continuity of life. All the energy is directed towards this continuity and towards the oneness of the idea. Activity and infinity characterize that oneness. That is why great art is never tight and closed-in, but reflects the might and majesty of space.

There is much acceptance of the new art and many think the old art passé. We want to enjoy and learn from the good art of yesterday and today. Great art includes but rises above and beyond the contemporary into the eternality of the universal. Great art is not superficial or manneristic, it is honest and basic and speaks to all mankind.

The masters have put depth and understanding and life in their work so that the best of their art keeps unfolding with newness. We must give time to allow ourselves to receive as well as to express. We have to wait and listen for that which speaks to us of the universal. All great art expression is involved with the control that emanates from the law of oneness. Great art is not geographic, detached or exhibitionistic; it is inclusive, all-embracing and uniting. Great art has profundity combined with spontaneity, buoyancy, and balance.

18

Ultimately, the greatest art rises above complexity so that it touches you with the simplicity of its feeling. It may appear uncomplicated and may leave you with the feeling that "I can do that."

A great work of art resolves into equilibrium, harmony, and a sense of eternity.

Great art is involved with a reality which breathes and loves and liberates. The response to art in nature is deep in the heart of all people. All men react to the beauty of a sunrise and to the wondrous forms, color, and movement in nature. Nature helps to open the consciousness to the love of creativity. It speaks of mightiness and tenderness, movement and quietness.

The highest art has an underlying quality of warmth and love and life. The artist has an heightened awareness of the infinite nowness of experience.

PAST AND PRESENT ART. We learn from the past but we do not repeat it. Creation is from an infinite source, infinitely expressed; therefore, it does not repeat itself.

Great artists are seldom recognized in their locality and in their time. Cezanne received dreadful criticism. Rarely was anyone so slandered by the critics. They were not prepared for his originality and for his profound and individual expression. Cezanne developed a new understanding of the flow of space that unites and envelops all the constituents of a painting. He became the father of modern art and paved the way for an abstract reality rather than for literal representation. He prepared the path for more comprehension of basic principles and for new thinking, thus breaking barriers.

Cezanne had little thought of success. Like Vermeer, he had scant acceptance in his lifetime. Today, he stands as a liberator in the approach to art and as one of the giants of all time.

Today's art may, or may not, evolve from the art of the past. But if it is good art, it observes principles similar to the art of the past. Art never repeats because of the nature of its infinite source.

CHAPTER TWO

THE INDIVIDUAL IN ART

UNIVERSALITY. The individual is one who is timeless, complete, and has all within himself. He has grandeur of feeling. He feels the wonder of man and of nature. He respects and appreciates the nobility of man and the vastness of the universe as God's creation. It is the individual that leads the way.

What counts for the individual? Adventure into the unknown. Why leap into the unknown? The desire to express the deepest freedom.

We have to exercise our individuality, get familiar with it, and be at home with it. Without the expression of individuality, there is no individuality. This individuality is unlimited. There has never been anyone like you and never will be anyone like you. To the degree that you respect your own individuality, you respect man's individuality. We cherish all individuality.

Forget ideas of background and environment. You are independent of them. We rise above our backgrounds and go to our hearts and know what we feel. Do not be afraid of your feeling. Fear will leave with patience and kindness towards oneself.

We must not allow others to tell us what to feel. Children who are told how to react become puppets and their power of individual expression is hampered. Without free thinking, there is no greatness. When one lends himself to mass thinking one must be aware that the thinking may not be his own.

Individually, we have something to project. It is constant newness—every day is wonderful. Being true to oneself is the path to self-confidence. We cannot repeat the past, even our own, for that is limitation. Repetition lacks the living quality which is in the newness of the present.

You do not try to become individual—when you are truly natural it necessarily follows that your painting is individual.

There is no end to the creative approach in painting. Giotto, Piero della Francesca, El Greco, Rembrandt, Cezanne, Van Gogh, Matisse (to mention a few) do not have to sign their names. Each of us has the gift of individuality. There are specific categories with specific characteristics, but within these are individual variations.

Individuality must be cherished and respected in oneself and in others. There is nothing as wonderful as the individual in that he has his own niche in eternity and no one can replace him. The artist is an individual thinker and not a peg in a scheme.

The individual is the most powerful force in the world.

BEAUTY. Beauty is fundamental to the activity of truth. One has the power to express beauty and if one denies this, he denies himself. He denies the joy that frees the spontaneity of expression. We must let the inner sense of beauty soar. We must increase our sense of the beauty of the universe. We are not creating this sense, we are born with it. Freeing our sense of beauty releases a sense of harmony. It is there and needs to be freed. We known within when we are in tune.

Beauty is independent of dimension or age. Poetry is an innate quality within us. We must take time to feel this, and we must try to please this inner feeling. Never tell another person how he should look at a painting. We are all seeing individually. Who can say red is more beautiful than blue, or vice-versa?

Bach was involved with the universality of beauty, the glory and the truth of life. Bach's music expresses the greatest of organized beauty, the greatness of spirituality.

The more you feel beauty, the more you reflect it. If you are reaching out, if you would like to share, let these desires take over. The path will open.

You must become aware of what touches you, of what is meaningful to you, what gives you a sense of beauty. Many are searching. Mozart believed in beauty with a conviction which he developed into timeless glory.

Experiencing a sense of beauty in the present step invigorates and accelerates the next. Feel the beauty in relationships and proportions. What you do, no one else would do.

There is no beauty without order. True art reflects the life-giving order of the infinite universe. The controlled repetitive order of material design may be of use, but is separate from the deep quality of art. The order in art is involved with the living, breathing, dynamics of space. When the life quality is not maintained in a painting, the beauty you started with is destroyed. Beauty is the reflection of the living order of the universe. An expression of life cannot be outlined in a tight container. How beautiful things appear because of their arrangement in space. Life, freedom, beauty are realities.

RECOGNIZING YOUR OWN GIFT. A teacher does not make an artist. A teacher does not put anything into you, but helps to bring forth that which is your natural endowment. Your latent talent needs guidance and nourishment. Learning does not make the artist. It is practice and effort that comes from the heart and from the intuition that makes for one's development. The teacher can help your growth through inspirational approaches that deepen your understanding and stimulate your interest.

The artist works with positive forces and ideas. The ideas are always subjective and demand entire concentration for their fulfillment.

Work in your own way and know what you are looking for. The artist is sustained by using his own intelligence and mind and heart. When we are completely ourselves, ideas come clearly and we can express them. These are great gifts—awareness and clarity.

The great artist does not consciously create a style, but he feels he must express deeply his conviction. His conviction creates his style. The wellspring of life takes over. There is always the new day and the new experience. The child-like enthusiasm refreshes. It means oneness and uncomplication. This is what the artist needs.

It is necessary for the artist to respect and nourish his own gift.

LOVING AND GIVING. We are not likely to love a painting that is not loved by the artist who painted it. The artist in his heart embraces everyone and feels enveloped by beauty. Those who give the most have the most expansive and most inclusive love in their hearts. Compassion and generosity make them want to share the joys of creation. The artist lifts us into another world when he gives forth this meaningfulness. The music of Mozart and Bach is full of joy and compassion.

When listening to a musical performance, we know the music wishes to come through, not the nervousness of the artist or his sensitivity to others, but the pure music must come forth. The artist works in the direction that allows his expression to be heightened. We must be patient with our development. When we sense an idea, we must nourish it with love. An idea works out if we do not limit the time and wedge it in with impatience. Dedicated thought is needed. Gratitude for the experience and for the growth in understanding lubricates the way. Give power to what you know and not to what you do not know. Our deep desire is to express the wonder of life.

.

CHAPTER THREE

OUR RELATIONSHIP TO ORDER

INSPIRATION. Our need is for inspiration. If we seek it, we find it for it is always available. Inspiration and work go hand in hand. Painting is a job that needs patience. Be at the job and the inspiration comes. Be ready for work, for the inspiration may come at an unexpected moment. It may come at an odd hour. Have your mind and your materials ready.

Inspiration may express itself in an unexpected way. Not a labor. Prepare your attitude, but not the expression, for that is spontaneous. Without warmth and life there is no art. Art is not manufactured. It is born. All inspiration is combined with control. When something touches you, dwell on it. It will help to inspire you in your own direction.

The artist has a direct path. Beethoven sustains us with the reality of glory or we could not soar with him. If we share the great depth of his experience we can soar.

That which comes from love is not laborious. When music or literature seems laborious, we know it was not approached with love and joy. Love and joy free the qualities of spontaneity and lavishly use space.

HARMONY, FEELING. The creative artist has his own recompense, his own inner glory, even though he may not have public success. In order to shed forth this glory, he must have it first in his heart. The work is to stir up the heart and to let the talent take over.

We let go and trust our talent. If we sincerely like an idea, we are likely to include it in our art work. If we feel deeply drawn to it, we can make it magnificent. If we are harmonious, we are free to learn and to change and to progress.

There is a difference between spontaneity and impulse. Spontaneity is effortless, innate, a natural wellspring within one, stemming from equilibrium. Impulse is likely to be sporadic, tentative, stemming from excitement, tension, or induced stimulation.

Recognize when you are harmonious. You are then ready for your art work. You are in tune, embraced in the beauty of infinite space. The vast sense of what exists in the universe flows into the movement of the painting.

We cannot be artists until we acquire this sense of harmony. It is a quality of the great universal rhythm which is not possessed when we are in a rush, hurried, or anxious. When we are part of this rhythm, we reach people. It is natural to be in this great rhythm.

Ask yourself: "Why am I working like this? What is the meaning of this painting?" There must be gratification in it. When one feels harmony, one rises above the personal and feels a sense of great truths.

THINKING AND VISION, SEEING. Artists are thinkers. What does the artist think? What does he want to paint? The thinking is not from the textbook, it is from the heart and the spirit. The great artist does not repeat or imitate what he did yesterday, for today comes with a freshness of inspiration. His thinking rises above the temporal into the timeless.

The world has grown familiar and small so that there are hardly any shocks left and not much left to do with new paint tricks. We seek honest painting. Depth of feeling demands depth of expression.

Ideas force the creation of technique for their expression. The artist is always asking himself: how can I express the idea that is so alive to me? The desire to express this aliveness forces the technique. This is proved in the painting of Van Gogh and Cezanne where the feeling created a new method of application of paint.

When we come into a room, we sense the environment including the person or persons. What we sense is what counts and is what comes out. We remember the atmosphere, what we felt, and that is what we recall when we paint.

Sometimes our vision gets stuck, as a record gets stuck—and is not really ours—and we must change it. We must be free to be led to new paths. Let us see as though we have never seen before.

A plant or a tree may inspire you. If you love it, you wish to give it space. You can see with your inner vision. What you feel when you see will project into your painting.

There is no limit to your vision. When you have a vision, this wants to come forth. Your vision is at one with inspiration and ideas. You do not have to come under the pressure of "should" or "ought to". It is wonderful to have the simple joy of activity as a child does.

The astronomer looks to the sky with one vision, the artist with another vision. An horticulturist gives a botanical name to the flower, but the artist is interested in what the flower conveys in forms and relationships. The artist has a sense of inner light. He does not have to see it. He knows the light is there. Beethoven did not physically hear his music.

Ask yourself: "Am I going in this direction or that? How can I improve?" . . . "Is my thinking liberating or is it in the bind of imitation? Am I caring for my work so that I approach it with enthusiasm or am I approaching it as a stepchild or chore?" Any doubt you feel will project a negative feeling to your expression.

Forget the outside world. Let the natural energy flow. We cannot worry over what others say. Listen only to those who speak sincere knowledge or from a genuine interest in your progress. Be alert that nothing robs you of your rightful joy in what you are doing. We often rob ourselves by self-condemnation and impatience. We can learn from the five-year-old who is eager, observant, wholehearted, and oblivious of others.

When we express with a spirit of ease and love, we have the essential of art.

ORDER. Have you ever lain on the grass and looked up into the stars? They go an into infinity. No matter how many there are, each is maintained in its rightful place. All stars and planets exist in the great spacial order of the universe. We have a peaceful, orderly creative mind inspired by beauty and the infinitude of expression. Quietly, we can feel our belonging. Timelessness cannot be expressed without universal love and a universal sense of order. The eternal spacial order is reflected in the spacial order of great painting.

CHAPTER FOUR

THE PREPARATION THAT SUSTAINS

TOOLS. The poet's tools are of language and speech. The artist's tools are visual. Both are involved with feeling the reality of timeless beauty. The ancient Chinese artist gave himself time to feel space, quietness, poetry, and universal beauty.

The painter uses all the means available to express what he feels. Color is his tool, it is with color that he enters space. His understanding of color relationship grows deeper and deeper. He feels the power of the dark and the light and he allows himself to make this as expressive as possible.

You are the master and can choose the way to apply the paint or any other medium until you are satisfied with the achievement. You can keep on changing your painting or you can make an entirely new work. The artist works with unlimited possibilities.

PREPARATION. Prepare your attitude, but not the expression, for that is spontaneous. We are not under pressure to make an accomplished painting, for we are learning by degrees. To the child, self-expression is natural and he does not sit in judgement of himself. The more receptive one is, the more one receives. Our responsibility is to be receptive to the growing experience. In "Hamlet", Shakespeare says: "The readiness is all." Real dedication to even a single experience gives power.

Allow the idea for your work of art to come in a simple, natural way.

Encourage yourself to feel warm and appreciative of your own idea. The more joyous and enthusiastic you feel about the ideas of your work, the more prepared you are for the expression.

We must know about our materials. Have your materials organized and easily available so that you are ready when the desire comes. Declare the nature and potential of the medium.

We start with an empty canvas. Only that which is in our thoughts and feelings can happen. We react to infinite ideas, infinite life, infinite space, infinite energy, infinite love. Our work is not laborious. We are not burdened.

Contemplation is desirable. Contemplation prepares the way for communication. It helps to maintain the oneness of thought that holds all the parts in place. We solve problems by getting outside of them. The potter is not in the clay. All parts must support the oneness of the idea. The parts cannot take the leadership. Not impulse and emotion, but the wisdom of universal rhythm allows all to fall into place.

We are called upon to use our higher capacities. The great musical performer may have a long practice period, but when he is playing he lets his talent take over with spontaneity and brilliance. It is the same with a painter.

Love your activity, use the opportunity of your free moments as well as longer periods of time. We must work and we must love our work. Sentiment is not enough.

DISCIPLINE. We have a need for quietness so that we can receive and digest. Contemplation releases the talent. The release is such that one feels as though one dances as one works.

We wish no locked doors, mentally speaking. Life is unlimited, so we have looked doors only when we ourselves create them. An unfinished drawing where doors are not closed is better than one that has been forced to a tight finish. Take your work only as far as the feeling takes it. Little children understand this.

Know what is meaningful to you. There are no rules, but there is immense discipline in creativity. We are in the universe and we include the universe in our thought.

We set the mood by the first few things that happen. We cannot see the leaves actually growing, but we see the full blossom as evidence of the continuity of growth. And so it is with our progress. If we stay in the unity of the whole, how can we go wrong? Be loving in every line, stroke, area, relationship. A loving attitude always involves patience.

The all-inclusive oneness of the brotherhood of man must be in our consciousness. Then our performance is not a solo virtuosity, but an expansive, embracing unfoldment. Rejoice if one of you exhibits. One may be more ready to exhibit than the other.

With humility, we empty ourselves of previous ideas and know that life is all-important, the universe magnificent.

The discipline is to let our feelings become more pure and more simple.

INTUITION. Without intuition there is no art. No accumulated knowledge can substitute for intuition. Intuition helps you to build from your experience. Intuition is not mysterious, it is innate intelligence—mind. Intuition guides and analyzes for you. Without intuition we have nothing.

Intuition is always available. It never repeats in the same way. Artists trust intuition. Value yourself. Value your innate intuition. It is an endowment which is more permanent than momentary inclination. Intuition is at war with conventional beliefs. Trust your intuition and get away from stereotyped conventions.

We can be eaten up by doubt. But we learn to exercise the faith of our intuition. We must try, and we must allow for failures, for we learn by mistakes. We are not fair to ourselves if we do not allow a margin of error. Your natural intelligence is helping to free you. Our intuition leads us to progress and unfoldment. There is a great blessing for those on this path.

Some artists have a marvelous period and then peter out. Cezanne became greater. Mozart had continuous unfoldment. Equilibrium usually accompanies intuition and protects from false influence and over-stimulation.

Intuition takes over as you lend yourself to its guidance. You feel your painting expanding. An innate quality within you is called forth that makes you know when the space flows. We cannot partake of anything to the fullest extent unless we have participation. The power to relate is an intuitive gift and gives us a promise of beauty.

We juggle between what we feel and what we know. Intellect and intuition are a necessary powerful combination. Intuition comes first and the intellect gives power to the intuition. It may take time for your intellect to catch up with your intuition. That is why we must trust our feeling and put our painting away for a while, rather than destroy its creativity with unfeeling mental knowledge. Love is the greatest power, try to love your activity.

In our chapter on painting under the heading Freedom, we talk on how the mental and the intuitive serve one another.

CHAPTER FIVE

DRAWING

PURPOSE. Drawing is usually a black application on a white surface. Crayons and other color mediums are used. Drawing is expressed with a concentration on line and outline but also may include mass areas and textures. As in every work of art, a drawing is directed to the infinity of space while bringing out a specific idea. Drawing often has structural value. The drawing experience is important for the artist. It is likely to be an unconscious element in freeing him to have a more substantial painting experience. While serving this further purpose, it has its own legitimate beauty.

Our progress in drawing is always in the direction of feeling life. Constantly, we are relating to the life movement of the total work. The machine is prescribed, but the human can express an infinity of relationships. Human movement first happens in the mind. We get up because we first think of getting up. This thinking is usually intuitive and subconscious. It is the same in drawing.

The importance is to feel. Something that feels right makes drawing a natural thing. While drawing the figure, feel that this is the most interesting, the most dynamic experience in the world. There is a tendency these days to belittle the eternal human experience. Art reveals a newness and individuality of attitude. One can never cease to marvel at the eternal wonder of the creation of nature. How can we ever cease to marvel at the form and movement of which man is the living embodiment? We look beyond the physical appearance

to sensing that which breathes and feels and is eternally related to space.   Feel
the great humanity in Rembrandt's drawings.   They show his never-ending
patience, his control, his spontaneity.   Acquire for yourself a book of his
drawings and find the pleasure of knowing them intimately.

LINE – OUTLINE.   The artist is involved with an unfettered rendering of
a living experience.

The line is man's way of animating his art expression.   The line and the
outline belong to art and are derived from nature.   The line that is outlining the
object is also outlining the space.   It affects the dynamic whole of the composition.   What makes us put a line here or there?   It is a tool to help our expression
and may be used delicately and splendidly.   The outline often gives the desired
fine enunciation.   The line may serve to accentuate or contrast mass areas.

We use line or outline when it serves the development of the total space.
The line belongs as much to the space as to the form.   The line indicates what
is happening to space.   So think of line as belonging to space.   This is important for our development.

It is the spacial need of the drawing that leads us to use either a continuity
of line or a broken line.   It is expressiveness that we are aiming for.   We hold
onto the total idea and that helps everything to fall into place in a natural way.

Look at Van Gogh's "Berceuse."   Expressive as a painting.   The woman
bursts into flowers.   The lines come out of space.   There is no cramped area,
for no matter how small the area, it reflects infinity and is contained within the
infinity of the total space.

Matisse in his line drawing generates life and space.   He projects from a
feeling of joy the quality of an infinite and large world.

As each shape or line goes down, it must relate to the depth of the whole
and be on one plane and relate to what has gone before.   The smallest line
must be felt as necessary to the whole.

We can project through the power of the line.   Line and mass can be
adjusted to serve the oneness of the totality.   They are carried on the movement
of the rhythm of the totality.   Being necessary to the total is what makes the
line significant.   Bring to the drawing the spontaneity, intelligence, and life that
we see in Rembrandt's glorious contribution.

CHAPTER SIX

PAINTING

FREEDOM. We paint with freedom. Have such inner dedication that your individual thinking cannot be dampened. Be responsive to the new, but at the same time stay with that which feels right to you. When we lose that which feels right, we become stymied. Fear steals our powers away. What we know today is enough for today. Tomorrow is another experience.

We have ideas. Ideas are thoughts formed with beauty and principle that become channeled and complete as we work with dedication. We have to start with a sense of freedom for what we feel and for that which is important to us. We do not force ideas—we allow them to come. They stem from infinity and are given expression by the individual. The power of a right idea can live forever.

Progress is always in the direction of liberation. We aim for freedom and control. When we put down what we feel, that is freedom, and the control is trusting this. Joyousness accompanies freedom. You are in the driver's seat—can shift and change within the total or you can change your ideas entirely. With spontaneity and freedom, you become open to the new idea. There are so many ways of seeing. Our vision should not become stereotyped. We must do what is helpful to us. If our work is approached as a chore, it will lack the living quality. It is intelligent to be free. A talent wants to be expressed. It is nourished by the attitude that it is a pleasure to work.

We do not build the whole from the parts, but start from the oneness of

the idea within which all flows. We are always seeking more light and more buoyancy.

Control is the holding on to the one idea, thereby steadying and freeing the organization. Control depends upon the clarification of the idea and the purification of the feeling. The mental and the intuitive meet. If only mental, there is danger of mechanization and lack of individuality. If only intuitive, there is not enough knowledge to support the growth.

If we are in the rhythm of joy and feeling, we do not tire. We seek the flow and rhythm of relationships. You cannot be touched by crushing circumstances when you feel like a bird that can fly above them. We learn through revelation, and at the same time we are analytical in our thinking.

We want to support that which helps our growth and we do not settle for mediocrity.

LIGHT. Light is a power that meets the need of mankind. Let us think of light as clarity and order. To the artist, light is an inner as well as an outer experience. Cezanne uses light as a great force. The light in his painting has a flow of continuity.

We relate to the sun. We find the blackest shadows when the sun is at its brightest. The white light of the sun includes all colors and is the source of all energy. Outside, all is painted in light which comes from the sun. Unlimited light shines through nature. Your capacity to sense light is unlimited.

The life quality coexists with light. Light is basic. Plants cannot live without light. Life is dependent on light. Light and understanding unite. Even in physically dark places we say: "I see", because within us we can have a light of understanding.

We are on the right approach when we learn to let the light take the lead in our painting. The light of the sun feeds the world, maintains man, animal, and vegetation. The artist has a sense of inner light. He knows the light is here. He does not have to see it. The inner vision of the artist gives him a sense of reality that helps him to rise above limiting circumstances. There is something immensely great about those who capture and live and project the living quality of light; it is this eternality of light that makes art timeless.

The light in your painting moves in rhythm.   Light is the positive force. Light takes over and has the initiative.   Light energizes.   Light is self-assertive.   Darkness is the non-entity, the absence of light.

Since nothing is negative in the life quality of painting, even intensely dark colors are so used that they project their own light.

Be inventive in creating light.   Relationships and contrasts bring out light. The powerful movement of light brings it more into evidence.   There are many ways.   Each artist finds his own.   The more intensely you feel light, the more deeply you penetrate into space.   All is feeling, no cold-blooded technique.

Think of the joy of light.   The more brilliant the light, the more the contrast of the shadows.   The more brilliant the sun, the more brilliant the darkness of the shade.   The artist cannot produce light, but he can produce the effect of light by way of color.   Light is produced in the shifting movement of color.   There is no method or formula for this, but we do have the power to project what we envisage and experience.   Children do this naturally.   They are drawn to the light of bright colors and the drama of contrasts.   The adult can add to this the depth of his experience.

Man reacts to the glory of light.   Rembrandt was interested in light emerging from the dark.   Cezanne was interested in light by way of color. Matisse went further than anyone with pure color in the expression of spacial volume.   Matisse was asked: "What do you think the coming generation will be mostly interested in?"   He answered: "Light."

Our aim is to use color to translate light.

COLOR.   John Ruskin said: "The purest and most thoughtful minds are those which love color the most."

Color is a tool with which to enter space and with which to express an idea.   The white paper or canvas provides the opportunity for all color. Nature is the greatest colorist and craftsman.   Every butterfly is fantastic in color, in design, and has its own character.   Nature does not hold back.   With sublime opulence, she gives us blue skies, azure waters, brilliantly colored flowers, birds, and other creations, with infinite variations.   We can marvel at the daring and elegance and infinite variation of nature's form and color.   The beauty of nature breathes with life and immortality.   Nature nourishes us lavishly with her beauty. A single flower speaks to us of nature's fabulous color.

No two artists feel the same about color combinations. By way of his thinking and feeling Cezanne used his color relationships to control the movement of his painting.

To Matisse, color is not just color but is a joyous unrestricted world. He exercised profound understanding in his use of color to project form and space.

One function of color is to make us feel the power of light. A painting is a world of color, form, freedom. Painting is very profound; using the color to project light-dark contrasts, textures, forms and space, we use color with balance and proportion.

We strive to develop an understanding of what color can do. This must be learned through intuition and experience and not through the theories or charts in a textbook. Many books are written about color, mostly unrelated to the aesthetic experience that acquaints us with its infinite expression. We are born with the capacity to feel color. We can feel different colors on one plane. Feel tenderly. What we appear to see and what we feel are two different things.

The first area of color is the most influential. It will influence what follows. Each color and shape must help every other color and shape. One color enhances another, suggests both power and gentleness. It should always come from the heart.

There is an inner ear within oneself. Beethoven proved this. There is also an inner eye. The artist senses color before he puts it down. At the start he may say: "I wonder what colors I will work with." Intuition is his guide. Thoughtfulness is combined with a free reign of spontaneity.

Little children select their colors naturally, always knowing what is meaningful to them. We can choose our colors naturally and happily. We choose what we react to. There is mood in color. We are carried along by our original feeling, but we cannot put feeling into what may be already static. Mood is oneness. It is easy to start, but to hold to the oneness is the discipline.

Try to use your innate sense of color. Let go of the mental. Sense the whole dynamics.

In painting, all qualities live in tranquility. We can work with many or few colors, infinite combinations and gradations. We can compare this to the infinite areas, combinations and relations of musical instruments in an orchestra.

The color arrangements may be large or small. We work to make a composition. If the addition of a line or an area is unfriendly, it destroys what is already there. All must breathe together. We are working on a big, wide world on our canvas; we are feeling everything and helping everything. Color has no limitation in depth. The result we achieve does not depend on method. Darks help toward building up the sense of light. It depends on where we start to look whether one color seems to be in front of another. Seek to express what you feel. Self-discovery is a discovery of your own feeling. All true experience is a revelation of the self. That self includes the feeling for color.

The impressionists learned that color is marvelous and that color has its own entity. Cezanne went further and used color to express ideas and the spirituality of man. Critics called him crude and an insult to the intelligence. Those who are supposed to know are often the ones who are less receptive to new ways. Cezanne went on to develop great color and form symphonies.

A painting, essentially, has one dominant feeling. We apply each color with this awareness. We may lose the feeling and then we have to recapture it.

Forms, movement, harmony—everything we have ever seen that has had a true appeal has unconsciously been stored in our consciousness. We are constantly in a state of discovery.

Far different from the above color approach is the approach used for sensational purpose to attract the buyer by way of the billboard and commercial illustration. Color in painting goes beyond decoration. In a great painting, color is form and space breathing the eternality of life; it is not emotional excitement.

Color has the power to carry us on an upward surge of beauty that reaches sublime heights.

LIFE FORCES. Love is the life force of art. To be able to receive love and to give love is our natural endowment. A child paints, wholeheartedly without tension because he is not aware of what people think—only of what he feels.

The life quality in painting is expressed through animation, volumes coming forth and volumes going back, volumes rising and lowering—all is breathing movement.

Many of us have felt engulfed by difficulties in life, but as artists we can rise above this. We can call forth an innate love of activity, beauty, and form. The harmony and space in nature help us to feel a sense of balance and equipoise. We are the master when our thinking is peaceful and clear. The artist sheds the external, feels the inner energy, and every color becomes a volume.

The artist is at one with nature. The great lake, the great ocean, affects him with the vitality of its horizontal expanse. The artist is continuously reacting to a great propulsion from a great force, the force of creation. He feels the universal forces of the ebb and the flow, the rise and the fall of spacial movement. The artist arranges nature according to the laws of continuity and eternity that he wishes to feel in his painting. The artist does not build from parts. He keeps sensing the totality within which all parts are related. The tree is not more important than the forest.

Cezanne's awareness of spacial movement expressed by masses and shapes led to abstraction rather than literal representation. In his still lifes, forms are as dramatic as a great waterfall.

We start with an unlimited sense of space. The sky is a force upward, downward, and all around. Nothing is inert in that which is life. As we walk on the floor or level ground we sense the force of a strong horizontal supporting our seeming vertical activity. No one falls off the curve of the earth for the aliveness of the forces of space holds the earth, the planets, and man in place.

The life force exists. We do not create it. We reflect the life force and therefore our art reflects it. We feel the total and the parts fall into place. Earth supports us. Trees rise from it—up—up—flowers grow up. We are upright—and uprightness is our nature. Broken man is down. Life force is an "up" force. The mighty oak grows up and out expressing the force of life. Life takes over and the growing is effortless.

In art, everything pulsates with the breathing quality of life. It is our birthright to feel joy, beauty, and life. Life being infinite, there is nothing finite in that which is living. The life movement in painting never stops. We want to make our painting alive, open. At the same time that there is movement in depth, all settles on the equilibrium of one great plane.

Discover yourself. All is within you, not in geography or place. We are all here to express the glory that we envisage.

Life and warmth, hand in hand, make us feel we have something to give. Giving enlarges the feelings.

We cannot project what is not in our hearts. Every age can be an age of glorious productivity and growth. Continuing to grow, old age does not set in, talents develop. New ideas appear. The beauty of today is new just as today is new.

The great law is the law of continuity. Continuity of movement in depth, not always obvious. Real living is a state of infinite progress. Life cannot be put in a box and controlled. The world reaches up. We have compassion, but the energy of life resists dwelling on tragedy.

CHAPTER SEVEN

CONTENT OF ART

SPACE. All ratios, proportion, and action are in space. Space is one and we never go off base if we remember that all is contained in this oneness. It is infinite in width, infinite in height, infinite in depth. There is no starting point or ending—it just is. It is more important to feel these things than to say them. Feeling these qualities of space gives us a joyous sense of freedom, which means we can go anywhere, mentally speaking.

Space reflects life. Let us respect the gift of our individuality, and let our sense of space come alive.

There is freedom in space, so there must be depth. Let us be conscious now of the depth of space. We know that space is deep, take time to see and to feel it.

Our work is to make the invisible real. Sensing the reality of space, the artist translates the invisible into the visible. Making the invisible real brings glory and beauty. Space is real. Knowing this, what you want to say spacially about the object becomes more real. Detail is valid when it glorifies the total space.

We live in a world where we know that the earth curves, yet the immediate horizontal surface is one on which we walk upright and on which our tables and chairs do not slide. The horizon is the illusion of the meeting of earth and sky. The one sky is out there and here. It is space, it is infinity. Since it is the same space out there as here, in a sense the space moves. That which moves is alive. Space flows. Space is alive. Space is one, infinite, immeasurable. This understanding is of the utmost importance to the painter who, on a flat surface, is painting space. He is not painting a three-dimensional figure with a two-dimensional backdrop as is often seen in the classroom. He is painting a more than three-dimensional space, and all forms within this space will reflect the voluminousness of the space. The space does not stop. It exists in front of the form as well as around it. The painting is meeting the challenge of making space alive, and that which is alive is not in a three-dimensional box.

Planes move in space. Space is made of infinite planes. The movement in space gives a sense of shifting planes. A dancer projects a weightless movement supported by the weightiness of space. The duet of space and movement becomes an achievement. Movement not supported by space is empty and lifeless.

In choreography we feel the dancer penetrating the space on the stage. There is no dwarfing of movement when the freedom of space is understood. The greater the art form of the dancer, the more conscious we are of spacial movement, its freedom and its beauty.

Space moves with a great rhythm in every direction. Space pours down, lifts up, moves backwards and forwards, and flows with the grace of great curved movements. All forms are embraced in the rhythms of space and reflect the glory of its infinity.

Rembrandt painted man as inseparable from the universe. His paintings breathe with a depth of feeling that projects into the depth of space. Outline is not evident; instead, there is the imperceptible flow of shifting masses. We feel space in front of the figure in a Rembrandt and space behind and space within the figure. Perfect equilibrium, sense of eternality because complete harmony is there. His later paintings increase in strength, tenderness, and nobility.

The forces in the space of Cezanne's still life are the same as the forces in nature with its mountains and valleys. Nothing is isolated. Space is friendly. The objects reflect the qualities of space. Feel the harmony of the whole entity. The dynamic space is pouring down into the objects and holding them up. Look at Van Gogh's painting "Bedroom at Arles"—we can feel its depth of feeling, producing the depth of space.

There are two immense actualities we intuitively express in a work of art—infinity and space. Ceaselessly, and unconsciously, we stay with the greatness of unlimited space.

FORM. In art we think of form as a delineation in space of a mass area. Form relates to space in such a manner that the two unite in one world. Space and form support one another. Forms may be large or small, heavy or thin, solid or porous, always individual and meaningful in their relationship to the space. The beauty of a form is inter-related with the beauty of the space it engenders. Form and space are embraced in the rhythm of the infinite and are infinite in their variation. Dwelling in infinity prevents crowdedness and permits the form to reflect the same infinity. There is nothing automatic or ritualistic in the vision of the artist. New ways of seeing are being revealed to him. The artist, fervent about what is being revealed to him, expresses freshness and spontaneity, added to deep thoughtfulness.

We must patiently practice the drawing and the painting of forms until they are rightfully proportioned in their spacial relationship. Whether representational or abstract, forms must relate individually and collectively to the totality of the space.

A painting is the embodiment of form, space, and color, all conceived together, living in brotherhood. We paint from the point of view of oneness. Piero della Francesca, the supremely great artist, was a master of form and space. His figures, or groups of figures, became magnificent forms in space. Nothing seems difficult or laborious in his great mural in Arezzo where the forms are incredibly beautiful. Cezanne, another master of form and space, said: "Every form could be reduced to a cube, a cylinder, a sphere." Rembrandt, in his painting "Young Girl in the Half-Open Door", reveals how the space he paints creates the form. The form is not held within the boundary of an outline but comes to dramatic life through elements of contrast. Forms have the power to express ideas and thoughts as well as visual concepts. The forms in music reveal this power.

OBJECTS. No matter how beautiful, we do not paint objects as an end in themselves. Objects in a painting should reflect the infinity and power of space, and if they enhance relationships, we welcome them.   The objects serve to make us space-conscious.

We must release the entire space when we wish to include another object. Sometimes several objects form a unit.   As the space behind and in front is felt, volume is created.   While each object first relates to the total, it must also relate to the other objects.   We are working for integration—nothing crowded, nothing isolated—everything speaking for itself to all.   Then a radiance comes through.

Cezanne's space is expressed in volumes, and his objects are expressed in volumes and a spacial order which reveals itself in quiet drama.

Recall the Buddhas in the Art Institute.   They have perfect equilibrium with the upright of the torso rising out of the horizontal of the lower limbs. There is a rise of great planes, no matter which way the Buddha is moving.   The finest of the Buddhas invites us to enter a world of deep thought, a world of the equilibrium of the horizontal joined with the strength of the vertical, and an overall wisdom, graciousness, and compassion.

When arranging a still life, the objects should be related so that they have spacial vitality.   The objects may be meaningful to the artist, but their major importance lies in the extent to which they enhance the movement and beauty of the composition.   It is always the major idea that decides which objects are to be invited into the painting.

THE FIGURE.   The human figure is capable of the most exquisite expressiveness.   It becomes a potent medium in the art of the dance, of the drama, and in the expression of human emotion.   The body reflects moods and attitudes. It embraces countless curves and angles and related movements.   The hands and fingers relate to the total movement even though they are a small part of the entire figure.

The seated figure includes that which it rests upon; therefore, in a certain sense the chair and the figure become one unit.   However, we must remember that the inanimate chair can never take on the importance or the wonder of the alive human being resting upon it.

With a standing figure, the full weight is on the feet.   With this firm support, we feel the figure can sway, bend, and reach up very high.

44

A living human being reflects all the qualities of life—its rhythm, its continuity, its beauty. A figure may be in a lying-down released position, and yet suggest potential movement. In its balances and equipoise there is the dynamics of mind able to release unlimited activity.

Why do we want a live model instead of a mannikin? An inanimate entity can never replace that which is alive, even though the alive is in a state of rest. Ponder this and sense the wonder of that which is a living creation. That which is inanimate is a finite statement in contrast to the unlimited capacity of the living. The figure of the animal is of considerable interest and has its own magnificence, but it does not give us the communication that comes from the human which reflects a higher reasoning power.

In our art work, it is wise to start by trying to educate our vision to see with newness. Try to think of how a face looks to the baby in the crib. Think what it must be to see a nose, eyes, ears, for the first time. It might appear as hills, valleys, and eyes that are living pools of expression. Think of what hands and feet look like to one who has never seen a hand, or the strangeness of a foot. Think of the remarkable flow of limbs extending from the torso, the torso supporting the rising neck, and the beauty of the head flowing from the neck, all related in a great continuity. It takes courage to see the newness of that which is always with us.

There is no one without beauty, for each is the reflection of a consciousness that feels and thinks and moves. Thought rises above age, physical measurement, lends a dignity to every human figure.

Rembrandt in his portrait of "the boy" does not isolate the figure but involves it with the space so that the boy and the space become one. He is giving the invisible a visible reality—at the same time he is translating the visible appearance into invisible qualities such as dignity, graciousness, joy, etc. Since the vision can always be new, the stress need not be on new subject matter.

Matisse said: "To see is itself a creative operation requiring an effort." Let us make the effort to see, to look and to see with the wonder of a new vision.

CHAPTER EIGHT

GROWTH

EXPERIENCE. Today is a new day. We do not stand still, for experience is unlimited and progress is the law of growth.

Experience is individual. Letting go of the past opens the way for the new idea. Our courage invites advancement.

We decide on our approach and then we must be consistent throughout the work. Keep clarifying the painting, solidifying the idea, supporting it with more tenderness and strength. Desire to make it more meaningful. All the while our discipline is to keep feeling the totality.

Be patient with yourself. Try to love life and love your work. They go together. Talking about your experience may make the completion more difficult for yourself. Let the work speak for itself. We are having new experiences all the time and the deeper they become, the greater our capacity for more. We do not lean on another person but on the thinking that helps to strengthen our growth. We are discovering underlying universal principles. We must be alert for content. Is it meaningful, or is it just new, new, new? We look for the substantial and the universal and the permanent, rather than the sensational. Spiritual content is not easily recognized. It is that which moves us in Bach, Mozart, Beethoven, Cezanne, and a beautiful sunset.

We must give wholehearted attention if we wish to receive full value from the experience. Our steps toward it are valuable. We can have the spontaneity

of the child, but our motto is "work, work, work!" The more we think and do, the more clarified our experience. Only as we grow can we help another to grow. We always respect the individual.

We have a language that cuts across the barriers of time and race. The great art of the past communicates and is as real to us as the great art of today. It has been revealed that roses flourished on the earth some sixty million years ago. That makes a mere two thousand years very close and the renaissance practically like today.

We become broad in our understanding and we welcome a meaningful idea. In comparison with one's total capacity, even the more cultivated is still a beginner. With a quiet attitude, we become more receptive. Progress is a joyous experience.

EXPRESSION. It has been said that expression is the cure for depression. Joy is expansive and inclusive and is not dependent on material situations. When one's expression is right, no one can talk you out of it. This attitude makes for happiness and for fruition. This is not a rebellious but, rather, a confident attitude. You have the capacity for infinite expression within the framework of universal principles. Your own feeling invites your own living expression.

We are here to express our talents, our gifts for living, our gifts for love. Consciousness is not a vacuum. Therefore, fill it with that which is positive rather than that which robs you of inspiration. The negative cannot serve you. We allow the blossoming thoughts to develop into full consciousness so that we can utilize them. Our sincerity and right attitudes lead to freedom, self-confidence, and joy. We all know in our hearts when something is meaningful —something within tells us. Difficult to talk about, and almost too precious to ask about. Love is a presence that finds expression in giving and identifies itself with life. The plant has courage that it will live. It expands by an inner weightless force. So with our experience; it expands with an inner weightless force. The happy child lets go of yesterday; no weights, is receptive, open. We can learn from a child.

It is wonderful when painting projects a feeling of "surprise" as from the brilliant light of the sun; not shock, but a sudden sense of how wonderful, how

47

amazing reality is. Who cares for deadness or dullness? There is too much leveling of tastes and opinions. Too much stunt-seeking.

Do not worry that you may not repeat the good work you have done. Every day is new and ideas are infinite.

What do we wish to express? That is the search. Do not be afraid to go deeply into any new approach. Eventually you have to go to your heart. We do not wish a cliché of any kind. The newness of an idea shows the inexhaustibility of creation. Some seek newness in technical devices and innovations. This is a danger. What do they end up with? Tricks, superficiality, and a dead-end vogue. Seek the atmosphere that supports the inner strength. We cannot have two points of view at the same time.

Copying others lessens our own power of expression. The great battle every artist has is to be himself. It is simple, but not easy to be oneself. In the beloved words of Shakespeare: "To thine own self be true; and it must follow as the night the day thou canst not then be false to any man."

We can love the experience of others as well as our own. Comparisons inhibit us. Never go on the defensive, but have the humility to change. Each flower in the garden is blooming for itself. We make no comparisons. We want to see with our own eyes. We want our own experience.

In all history the technical experts usually have tried to squelch those who express from the heart. The wish to preserve the status quo is at sword's point with the fresh expression of the individual.

A good painting lives in any room.

THE JOURNEY TO THE UNIVERSAL. Artists rise out of the personal thinking which separates into the universal that says "all men are related." The artist is expressing the oneness of nature and man. The artist is expressing man's humanity to man. He has the openness of a child. He senses the immensity of the universe and the relationship of man to this immensity.

Some start with limited thought and try to accomplish great art. Impossible. Work from the sense of the greatness of the universe.

Matisse said, "When I paint, I am with God." He said he was himself at that time, totally free then. Bach wrote at the end of each musical composition: "For the glory of God."

Art elevates the feeling—soaring, uplifting above the personal into universal grandeur.

Our capacities are released as our thinking broadens. We cannot sustain or support wisdom unless we know we are bigger than anything we do.

END OF PART ONE

PART TWO

APPROACH TO EXPRESSION

There is the beginning acquaintance with materials, but the advanced artist will find profound awareness released and exercised in the further approaches. The value of these approaches is in proportion to the time given to feeling intuitively.

VICCI SPERRY

CHARCOAL

Persistently and patiently they worked on the principles and exercises so necessary to the growth of their expression (p. 16).

CHARCOAL is a rich plastic medium. When kept sharply pointed, it can make a fine line drawing. Used with a broader point, it can produce mass areas of different textures. Compressed charcoal produces a very powerful black, but a medium charcoal allows far greater freedom because it can be erased and changed. There is a medium charcoal that can produce an intense black. That is most desirable. Try many kinds and make your own choice.

Notice the beauty of a clear black line against the white paper. Make a thick line and then make a very fine line. Contrast the line with a very black mass, a lighter mass, a textured mass. Have handy a small chamois and a kneaded eraser. Try rubbing the charcoal with your finger, or the chamois, or the eraser—you can get any effect you want.

You can spend a great deal of time over a charcoal drawing. You are the master—changing, reorganizing your drawing until it is as you desire, or destroying it and making a new one.

Make a composition of simple shapes filling the paper with various dark and light areas. The most dramatic contrast exists between the pure white and the deepest black.

Charcoal is richly satisfying because of its plasticity.

There is a tendency to think we have outgrown certain mediums—charcoal always has its unique, free and flexible purpose at any stage.

MOUNTAINS

Form relates to space in such a manner that the two unite in one world (p. 43).

THE artist is deeply involved with space. He is making visible the space which seems to be invisible. When he gazes upon the sheet of paper, some magic is going on in his consciousness. He no longer sees a two-dimensional paper. He is entering a three-dimensional world.

It is marvelous to see what the various heights of the mountains do to the infinite space of the sky. We feel the descending space greeted vigorously by the rising volumes of dramatic moutain shapes. The embrace of the sky envelopes the soaring mountains—lifting man into nature's glorious grandeur.

The mountains are great volumes of solidity enfolded in the contrasting volumes of living space.

Art is the reflection of feeling in which everything is related to the total space.

STILL LIFE — OBJECTS IN SPACE

No matter how beautiful, we do not paint objects as an end in themselves (p. 43).

NOTICE the dynamics of the relationships of the objects to one another and to the entire space. Feel the space pouring into the objects, supporting them and uniting them. Space is a living reality, nothing is inert within that living reality, for good art is a reflection of life.

We begin to feel rhythms in the various relations. Dwelling too much on the appearances of objects may stop the flow of movement. Feeling space helps to place and relate forms to the total composition.

With every approach, something of the vitality of the movement in space is being revealed.

HOW THE INDIVIDUAL SEES THE FIGURE

The body reflects moods and attitudes. It embraces countless curves and angles and related movements (p. 44).

TODAY, we will enjoy drawing the beautiful flow contained within the oneness of the figure. We are conscious of the vertical space created by a standing position, or of the horizontal space by a lying-down position. We become sensitive to these forces like the grass stretching out and the rising of the trees. Man is upright against the horizontal of the earth.

Each one sees differently. Also, each day each individual sees differently. This is the infinite variation and unfoldment of vision.

Rembrandt in his painting, "Young Girl in the Half-Open Door", expresses beautiful vibrating space. The space creates the form. Here, he shows how space and form become one living entity.

In drawing the figure with line, think of the line not as the outline of the figure but rather as that which is uniting the figure and the space. The line may be continuous or broken depending on the individual expression. Let the figure flow freely throughout the composition. Dwelling on the total sense of space will help place the figure and the relationship of the parts of the figure.

Drawing invites the use of mass areas and of textures as well as line. Encourage spontaneity, the joy of spontaneity, nothing laborious. The figure and the space unite in the flow of movement.

THE ALL-INCLUSIVE FIGURE

It takes courage to see the newness of that which is always with us . . . There is no one without beauty, for each is the reflection of a consciousness that feels and thinks and moves (p. 45).

I HAVE found in my teaching experience that a great drama is set up by drawing the profile of a large head with the sheer line of the back of the head contrasting with the articulation of the profiled forehead, nose, mouth, chin, etc.

The drawing of the features is never automatic, the lesser cannot take precedence over the greater. Therefore, the features, if portrayed, must serve the flow of the entire work. It is better to have a few lines that relate than a realism that violates the totality of the form and the space.

Man will never cease to wonder at the beauty of the head.

Hands and feet can have much meaning for us. We may be touched by their usefulness, their service, and their present restfulness. The more familiar we become with parts of the body, the less timid we are about it. If we choose to leave out faces, fingers, or any parts of the body, we do so out of strength of choice and not out of weakness. It is very interesting to make a total composition of hands or feet. It is our feeling that makes everything simple.

IN THE PARK

It is practice and effort that comes from the heart and from the intuition that makes for one's development (p. 22).

LET us feel the atmosphere of a park. How good it is to see people in a park. Let us try to see these people as a unit group. We are also going to be conscious of trees. Here we are—in a beautiful green park with people and trees. Interesting relationships are being set up. The trees, embraced in space, the people embraced in space, the park embraced in space. A great deal of activity is set up by feeling those relationships. Even though we sense the people as individuals, we are seeing them as a group unit in the park, rather than scattered throughout the park.

Feel the quality or the essence of being in the park and feel this as your own living experience. When we feel everything related to the total space, all resolves into a sense of equilibrium. It is not representation that we seek, but the quality or essence of the experience.

TEMPERA

The love of color, life, form spurs the devotion and activity
needed for the concentrated effort (p. 17).

TODAY, we will get acquainted with tempera colors. It is stimulating to see the actual colors in the jars before us, and what beautiful brilliant colors they are! Instead of squeezing unseen colors from a tube, the jars of color invite you to an immediacy that spurs spontaneity.

Tempera is handled with water and with a sable brush. It can be used like transparent water color, but its natural character is opaque and of vivid intensity.

Choose four colors whose relationship you like. As a musician explores all the possibilities of four instruments in the creation of a quartet, you will explore the possibilities of the four colors you have chosen.

Have ready a large sheet of paper, a jar of water, and a rag. One brush is sufficient, not too small, of a good quality that can come to a point for the painting of a line. After using a color, the brush is washed in the jar of water, wiped, and ready for the next color. This becomes an automatic gesture. Later on in your experience, you can use as many brushes as you desire.

Now for our approach. We will apply the tempera in solid areas of color—large, small, or both. Experiment for a while with the relationship of the water, the brush, and the color. Experiment with a drier brush and a wetter brush. You will learn that the less water, the faster the tempera dries. You will acquire your own feeling for the flow of the tempera.

We are involved with color relationship. See what happens when you add white to each of the four colors. After this, mix two of the four colors together until you have run through every combination. Enjoy this. Take your time and get the feeling of the wonderful hues, nuances, and combinations that exist in the realm of color.

If you have used up your sheet of paper, start another one. You can begin to make your areas of color larger and feel them related to the total space. Thus a sense of composition combines with the exercise. This is just a "get-acquainted" with the potential of color combinations.

Do not try to store up any of these results in your memory, for within your own feeling is always the capacity to achieve any shade of color that you desire. The very fact that you desire it means that you can achieve it.

No two people relate color in the same way—each one of you is endowed with an individual gift for color. This gift must be tapped from your intuition. It is not from a chart or a book.

Tempera gives you the apportunity to express yourself with the greatest spontaneity. It meets the need from kindergarten through one's entire experience. Matisse, in his eighties, used it in his last works.

APPROACH VIII

THREE ORANGES ON DIFFERENT PLANES

The eternal spacial order is reflected in the spacial order of great painting (p. 27).

TODAY, each one of you will take your turn before the class.

The approach is with tempera. When it is your turn, each of you will place a large-size paper on the easel set up before us. Along side the easel is a small table with three oranges. Our subject matter will be a simple arrangement of these oranges. When you are before the easel, individually you will make a spacial arrangement of these three oranges. In other words, you will arrange your still life of three oranges and then you will paint your own arrangement. The one that is at the easel will receive the quiet support of the rest of the class.

As you are placing the oranges, feel that you are putting one deep in space, one in front, and one in between. Before you do this, make the placement in your mind. Now you are ready to paint the oranges in the depth of the space of the paper. The oranges should be painted one size. Your feeling may tell you to make them rather large. Keep feeling the depth of the space, the relationship of each orange to the total, and to one another. Trust your intuitive power to work on this as an approach in space.

Every approach in space cultivates the capacity to project the depth of space which is so much needed in painting. It is important to rely on your feeling and this may take time.

Whether you are the one before the class or the one that is watching, you will be actively experiencing the approach. You will feel a sense of quietness as a result of the concentration.

61

TROPICAL INVITATION

All great art expression is involved with the control that emanates from the law of oneness. Great art is not geographic, detached or exhibitionistic ; it is inclusive, all-embracing, and uniting (p. 18).

W E will forget that we are in a basement and that it is a cold wintry day. In your mind's eye, see the blue ocean, the bright sand of the beach, the tropical growth, the warm sunshine, and the gay figures on the beach. We become more and more quiet as we feel this tropical atmosphere.

We see many figures on the beach. Each figure is a solid mass of color—walking, lying down, sitting. These live human beings are reacting to the warmth and the beauty of the atmosphere. It is wonderful how, through feeling, you can project the essence of an outdoor experience. This is a joyous approach and the joy that you feel will project into the rhythm of the painting.

DRAMA ON A BEACH

The artist arranges nature according to the laws of continuity and eternity that he wishes to feel in his painting (p. 39).

AGAIN, we will forget that it is a cold wintry day. As in the previous approach, we are lending ourselves to a tropical atmosphere—to the warmth, the ocean, the sand, and the brilliant sun.

There are just two figures on the beach. They have been having a happy time in the bright sunshine. One has walked away and is now under a tree in very dark shade. In the bright sunshine, shadows are deeper and make for a powerful contrast. Let us draw the contrast of one figure in the brilliant afternoon sun and the other figure in the deep shade of a spreading tree. There is a very quiet peaceful feeling. It matters not whether we express abstractly or representationally—it is feeling and space that are our involvement.

The great artist lifts you into his world. Beauty is a reality. In the eloquent words of Ralph Waldo Emerson: "For the world is not painted, or adorned, but is from the beginning beautiful; and God has not made some beautiful things, but Beauty is the Creator of the universe."

LIGHT ON DARK, DARK ON LIGHT
COMPOSITION OF FIGURES

Organization in art reflects the universal law of oneness within which everything is related. Within this oneness, the forms and the space unite on the rhythm of the movement. More and more we allow ourselves to feel the depth of space (p. 17).

TODAY, we will draw with black India ink and a tempera brush. Take a large size sheet of paper, using it horizontally. Draw a faint vertical line dividing the paper into two parts. Mentally think of one part being dark and the other part light. Think of the figures we are going to draw as being light on the dark side, and dark on the light side. Bear in mind every moment that everything on either side is related to the total composition.

The model will give us several different poses. First, we will make a very free composition of several poses on the dark side; and then we will follow with several poses on the light side. Visualizing the space as dark will bring about its darkness and the figures will become vividly light. On the light side, the figures will be drawn using a dark effect, all related to the total composition. Our black areas are pulsating, living areas. Our light areas are also living, pulsating areas. Our composition is in the nature of a fugue in two parts, uniting and interweaving to project a breathing, living oneness.

Do not make this a formula.

STILL LIFE — INFINITE RELATIONSHIPS

When arranging a still life, the objects should be related so that they have spacial vitality. The objects may be meaningful to the artist, but their major importance lies in the extent to which they enhance the movement and beauty of the composition (p. 44).

TODAY, we will paint the still life before us, but before we do this, let us study this reproduction of Cezanne's painting of the still life with the apples and oranges on a fantastic white cloth uniting within a living drapery.

The apples are individual, yet become group units within the totality of the composition. Some of the apples are placed to give depth to the vast valley in the drapery. Throughout the painting, there is a weaving and inter-weaving of relationships and movement. The movement penetrates in many directions without limitation. As we look, we see more and more relationships.

In this painting we can feel a bigness and a monumentality, within which all the parts are embraced. The drama of the tablecloth, the beautiful flow of the drapery, and all the elements resolve into one great equilibrium.

Now work on the still life which we have set up for today. Notice how the total still life relates to the entire space, and then you can begin to see how each element of the still life relates to the entire space as well as to the other elements.

In all art experience, it is the vision and the understanding that is being developed. This prepares for the spontaneity of the expression.

S H A P E S   O F   L A K E S

The artist is at one with nature. The great lake, the great ocean, affects him with the vitality of its horizontal expanse. The artist is continuously reacting to a great propulsion from a great force, the force of creation (p. 39).

USE a large sheet of paper and just one color—blue tempera—any shade you desire.

Find yourself in a place in the world where there are thousands of small lakes of infinite shapes. The areas of land between the lakes are sometimes much narrower and smaller than the lake areas. Visualize this. Feel the atmosphere of lakes all around and on each side.

Start by painting a blue shape representing a lake. Develop a shape with sensitivity, working from the center outward. Now paint another blue shape of a lake, allowing room for many more, feeling the space is guiding you as to the size and shape and placement of the shape. It is your feeling that is producing the expression.

Spend time with each new shape. Do not leave it until you are satisfied with it. Every new shape is friendly to its neighboring shapes. Thus, with the added shape, what is already there is not destroyed. Let go when you feel your composition is complete.

This approach helps you to become more conscious of the flow of space that contributes so greatly to painting. This should never become a static or routine approach, for at every moment of our development in art, it is necessary to work from feeling and intuition.

MORE SHAPES — MORE LAKES

Do not be afraid to go deeply into any new approach. Eventually you have to go to your heart. We do not wish a cliché of any kind. The newness of an idea shows the inexhaustibility of creation (p. 48).

OUR approach today is similar to the last one—again we will paint small lake areas. However, this time we will use different colors of blue—green blues, purple blues, and also cobalt blues. Develop each shape with contemplation. The color of the shape may vary, but for this particular approach it is better to have no variation within the shape. Coax the areas into the shape you want, and feel each new shape is enhancing all its neighbors.

Seek the color that meets the need of the space and meets the need of the shape. After making many shapes—many lakes—your intuition will tell you when it is time to stop. When you are finished, compare this approach with the previous one (XIII). Each has its value and each is contributing to your deeper experience.

STILL LIFE — PAINTING SPACE

Space moves with a great rhythm in every direction. Space pours down, lifts up, moves backwards and forwards, and flows with the grace of great curved movements (p. 42).

SPACE is not a vacuum. Space breathes and lives. The objects in space co-exist in vitality within the space.

The still life before us has been arranged and re-arranged to give the greatest animation and flow to the space it engenders. Let us feel the living relationships of each of the objects to one another while, at the same time, feeling the relationship of the total still life to the total space. And equally we will try to feel the relationship of the space to individual objects. Thus a flow of relationships is set up that calls for life and movement in many directions.

Generally, the tendency is to dwell more on objects than on space, but today the forms of space will take preference over the objects. Grandeur, life, and movement exist in the forms of space. The objects, although different, will reflect the same qualities as the forms of the space.

When you think space first, what you say becomes more alive. Space being alive, it moves, and therefore appears on different planes. The more space-conscious you become, the simpler it is for the organization to fall into place. You practice art with your intuition and your intelligence.

You are growing in your feeling for the flow of space. You are finding that you are gradually using color not so much for representation but for its spacial effect. This is adding to your sense of freedom.

68

SPACE RELATIONSHIPS
ANIMALS ON A HILL

*Great art is involved with a reality which breathes and loves and
liberates.   The response to art in nature is deep in the heart of all
people ; all men react to the beauty of a sunrise (p. 19).*

TODAY, we are going to concentrate on the beauty of out-of-door space
relationships.   All shapes exist in infinity and are part of a great universal
rhythm.

Visualize a green hillside on which is a group of animals.   Feel the peaceful
atmosphere of this country scene.   The animals may appear as horses, cows,
sheep, goats, etc.   The animals may suggest abstract shapes or may present
themselves somewhat representationally.   They may be scattered or they may
be in groups on the hillside.   The main thing is to feel how the animals create
beautiful shapes in interesting space relationships.   All is alive and pulsating in
the out-of-doors atmosphere.   The animals are giving us the opportunity to
animate the hill and the entire space with living, interesting forms.   The spacial
relationships bring the space to life and give to our painting the aliveness of a
work of art.

COMPLETE WORLD WITH ONE ELEMENT

All stars and planets exist in the great spacial order of the universe. We have a peaceful, orderly, creative mind inspired by beauty and the infinitude of expression. Quietly, we can feel our belonging (p. 27).

TODAY, we have a comparatively simple approach. Again, as in approach VIII, each student will take a turn working before the class.

We will concentrate on painting one great element like an imaginary sun or sphere, related to the space within which it is contained. We will make a complete composition consisting of this one painted sphere and the white space around it. The painted sun will relate in perfect balance to the surrounding white area. Something within you will tell you when this perfect balance is achieved.

Paint the shape of the sun gently from its center towards its full form. You will know when it has reached the dimension that is in satisfying relationship with the total space. You may vary the color of the large element, the sun—let it be of your choice.

This approach is of a fundamental nature, helpful to your experience.

It is an approach in space with a simple but powerful relationship. Again, we are reminded that we do not make a formula of an approach. Enjoy it as an opportunity for development.

OIL PAINT

Love of nature, of man, and of beauty are primary forces that desire expression (p. 17).

THE principle of color is the same for oil as for tempera. The manner of application differs, for each medium has qualities of its own. Usually, we use bristle brushes. Several at one time. Sometimes one can also paint with a palette knife, but the brush gives the greatest variation and fluidity of expression. It is the result that matters and, after much experience, one feels free to use anything for a desired result. Turpentine is generally used as the thinner and the cleaner of the brushes.

For our approach today, we will use five colors, including white. It is almost impossible to get along without the white color. As we did with tempera, let us work with different shapes of color and different degrees of application, thin and heavy—also with varying textures. Oil paint is the most pliable of the color mediums. It differs from tempera or the acrylics in that it dries slowly, is of a more plastic nature.

Today, we will paint on illustration board or heavy paper. At a later lesson, we will paint on canvas board or canvas. You will find that the paint relates differently to different backgrounds.

This approach is acquainting you with the qualities of oil paint. Take your time with it and enjoy it. Oil paint is an endlessly interesting and inexhaustible medium.

After a thorough acquaintance with oil paint it is well worthwhile to experiment with acrylic paint and to allow yourself the freedom of choice.

STILL LIFE — FORCES, SAME AS IN LANDSCAPES

The forces in the space of Cezanne's still life are the same as the forces in nature with its mountains and valleys. Nothing is isolated. Space is friendyl. The objects reflect the qualities of space. Feel the harmony of the whole entity. The dynamic space is pouring down into the objects and holding them up (p. 42).

W E will paint with oil colors today. We will approach our painting naturally and without timidity, for we have had helpful preparation with our tempera approaches.

Let us study this still life before us. Like the world outside, it is involved with forces. The forces in the space in the still life are the same as the forces in nature with its mountains and waterfalls. Nothing is isolated—all is embraced in the space. Space is a living and a friendly force. The objects reflect the qualities of the space-force. Feel the harmony of the whole entity. The dynamic space is pouring down into the objects and is holding them up. The forms of the space and the forms of the objects are contained within the rhythm of infinite space.

Thinking of infinity prevents crowdedness. There is nothing automatic in our vision. We are always seeing in a new way. No approach can become routine, for we always allow ourselves the freedom of a new way of seeing.

An artist paints the reality of timeless forces. He senses that space is activated by forces which he expresses in the depth of rhythmic movement. He feels the harmony that comes from knowing that forces exist—that he does not create them, that he reflects them. Blind impulsive action may make us feel as though we are doing something, but it will not lead us into the path of gentle understanding that makes for growth and true strength.

We are becoming more conscious of the total ensemble and its oneness. Everything contributes to the one idea.

Art is an expression of life, and life expresses itself through forces.

APPROACH XX

COLOR AS LIGHT — THREE COLORS

> *The light in your painting moves in rhythm. Light is the*
> *positive force. Light takes over and has the initiative. Light*
> *energizes. Light is self-assertive. Darkness is the non-entity, the*
> *absence of light* (p. 36).

CHOOSE three colors whose relationship you like. We are going to use these colors as areas that relate to the space and relate to one another. These areas will be approximately two inches (2″) on each side and will be detached from one another. Allow yourself to feel that these square areas (or we might call them objects) have the power of light. You are adding a new dimension to your art experience. Man cannot create light but he can effect light through color relationships.

First, we place one area in space feeling that it is related to the total. Then, we place the second color area so that it seems to enhance the light of the first color area. (Take time to feel in what place the new area is needed before putting it down.) Then, we place the third color area still deeper in space, at the same time feeling that it is enhancing the light of the two color areas already there. This continues until you feel that your composition has gone as far as it wants to go. You will find that you may be repeating one color much more than the others and that one or two of the three colors will dominate the composition.

This is an approach in space placement, combined with the consciousness of the color being translated into light. This may be accomplished with any

74

colors, light or dark. It is our consciousness of illumination that brings life to the painting. Although a form may be rendered by a flat area of color, it cannot be flat in feeling. We become sensitive to its life, its breathing quality.

Before putting down these different shapes, mentally place them on your paper, Calmness allows your native intuition to lead the way. You will sense the pulsating, breathing quality entering the composition.

There is no formula for the projection of light through color relationships. It is something that is individually felt and gradually experienced.

APPROACH XXI

THREE COLORS ON ONE PLANE

Space is one and we never go off base if we remember that all is contained in this oneness. It is infinite in width, infinite in height, infinite in depth (p. 41).

TODAY, we have a most interesting approach. Choose three colors that appeal to you in their relationship. We are going to paint fairly large rectangles of a similar size. They will not be detached. They will be touching one another. We start by feeling that the paper or canvas is a volume. It is not limited to two-dimensional, but is a volume that we feel we can enter.

First place a large rectangle of color deep in space. This next rectangle will be of a different color, felt still deeper in space, and uniting on the same plane as the previous rectangle. It will take a little time to sense this. Now for the third step. Choose a rectangle of color that can be placed deep in space and can, at the same time, join the one living plane of what already has been painted.

The painter works with the depth of space. He is entering space and at the same time he is maintaining the one great living plane on which everything unites.

It is wonderful to achieve this understanding. Artists work in different ways to achieve this. It makes for the necessary living-depth-movement but at the same time does not stray from the one idea and the one plane. Cezanne was aware of this. So was Matisse, Mondrian in his way, and Pollock in his way.

These approaches will help to free your talent. They will also give you a deeper awareness of what the master artists have accomplished.

APPROACH XXII

STILL LIFE — SPACE NOT A BACKDROP

Being true to oneself is the path to self-confidence. We cannot repeat the past, even our own, for that is limitation. Repetition lacks the living quality which is in the newness of the present (p. 21).

LET us study this still life before us. Have a warm attitude towards each of the objects. Know that the space is as important to the painting as the objects. The space has infinite depth, is enveloping the objects, and is not a backdrop. There is an inner play of form and space, space and form, within the composition. To the artist, the still life reflects the forces in the universe. The macrocosm and the microcosm reflect the same world. It is the one spacial universe, the one energy, whether we are working on a small or a large canvas.

Every area no matter how small, no matter how large, is equally important to the whole. As we sense the one great space moving towards us, within which the objects are contained, we are rescued from the possibility of painting space as a backdrop. In the works of lesser artists, we see a figure plus a background, or objects plus a background. The great artists help us to know that there is one space encompassing the fore-front as well as the back—space cannot be cut off to become a backdrop.

Space reflects life. Without life, there would be no movement. The static is the reverse of life. The great law is the law of continuity. This continuity in movement in depth is not always obvious.

Our approaches are bringing forth an increasing awareness and a greater capacity to see and to feel.

FOUR COLORS ON ONE PLANE NOT TOUCHING

Dwelling in infinity prevents crowdedness and permits the form to reflect the same infinity (p. 43).

CHOOSE four colors whose relationship appeals to you. Let us make a composition of flat rectangular shapes somewhat similar in size—detached from one another. Allow yourself to feel the placement of the first shape and then gently paint it. Do not leave it until you are satisfied with its size and location in relation to the total white area. The first shape must be very tenderly felt. Take your time. Whenever painting the shape, start from the center and work towards the outside. We do not start it with an outline that becomes filled in—instead, we mentally place a shape and allow it to become defined by unfoldment.

Now you are ready to paint the next rectangle. Choose the color that seems to be on the same plane with the first color. The rectangles that follow continue to maintain the one plane. Everything follows as a consequence of that which is already there. Watch how the white canvas is coming to life and is responding with a movement of its own as each area of color goes down.

We paint these rectangles as flat areas, but we feel them as volumes, for there is nothing flat in the reality of the universe. Everything you are painting has a breathing quality, therefore this approach cannot become mechanized. It must be felt. The one great plane is actually a volume and each area of color is felt as a volume. All is harmonious within the one infinite total.

FOUR COLORS — TO EDGE OF CANVAS

If our work is approached as a chore, it will lack the living quality. It is intelligent to be free. A talent wants to be express-ed. It is nourished by the attitude that it is a pleasure to work (p. 34).

THIS has a similarity to the previous approach (XXIII). We will again work with four different colors and four rectangular shapes. In this approach, however, allow each shape to come to, and include, the edge of the paper. We work with the same tenderness to develop each area of color, and again we work to maintain this one great plane. Allow the rectangles to be fairly large and of similar size.

In this approach, we have a feeling of the space pouring from the outside into the world of paper. Each rectangle is contained within the space of the painting and, at the same time, the painting is uniting with the world beyond it.

Every approach has its value and is a new adventure in the learning experience.

FOUR COLORS TOUCHING ONE ANOTHER

While each object first relates to the total, it must also relate to the other objects. We are working for integration—nothing crowded, nothing isolated—everything speaking for itself to all (p. 44).

OUR two previous approaches (XXIII and XXIV) were acquainting us with four colors in the rectangular areas that did not touch one another. Today, we will work with adjoining rectangles of four colors. As we feel these different colors deep in space, we will be uniting them on one plane.

First, put down one rectangular area of color. Feel that it is related to the whole area. In this particular approach today, all areas will adjoin and touch one another. The second rectangles will relate to the total space and to the already painted area. Every step should be patiently felt. This saves time in the end, for it saves reworking. As the rectangles continue, the colors begin to repeat, some more frequently, than others. We always go back to oneness and to working from infinity. In this approach, we try to keep the shapes evenly rectangular, for they are more likely to touch that way.

Continue until you are satisfied with your composition.

We are unlimited in our capacity to feel movement. We are entering a world of space and at the same time we are working on one plane. Within the unlimited oneness, each element is related to the whole and related to every other element.

If you love what you are doing, the understanding is quickened. You will not bring harshness to it. The rectangles, side by side, never appear crowded because each is moving in deep space. Be calm and allow the true self to blossom. The inner self comes forth with patience and gentleness. In art, we can comprehend but not always explain. The same is true of life.

APPROACH XXVI

_____

CONTINUITY OF ONE PLANE
USING EIGHT OR MORE COLORS

The order in art is involved with the living, breathing, dynamics of space. When the life quality is not maintained in a painting, the beauty you started with is destroyed. Beauty is the reflection of the living order of the universe (p. 22).

TODAY, our approach will be based on the continuity of the one great plane using eight or more colors. Again, we will work with rectangular shapes. They will be rather small. They will be attached to one another.

Our consciousness of starting from infinity gives us vitality and control. Each of us operates as a complete individual, each flower in the garden is blooming for itself. The beauty within each of us is that inner quality which gives forth radiance. This is the opposite from the outward shell which cannot radiate beauty.

All the movement in a painting is an inner movement. This inner movement is expansive and yet all inclusive.

We are aware that we start with an idea, and we are aware of the fact that space is infinite—within this infinity, there can be no "tightness". There are no "tight" spots in infinite space. We can soar, think, and move.

We are the reflection of infinity, therefore we are unlimited in our capacities. We have ideas we never dreamed we had.

Art is the reflection of that which is eternal, timeless.

Continuing to grow, old age does not set in; talents develop. Matisse in his eighties felt beauty and joy, reacting to the glory of light, and expressing this in the clear colors of his last works. Cezanne achieved depth from the relationships of great horizontals and verticals. His technique evolved from the necessity of the idea. The clarity of the idea forced the technique.

Art is infinite in its expression. This follows the fact that man is individual and, therefore, individual in his own expression.

LIGHT AS COLOR — STILL LIFE

*Nature does not hold back.   With sublime opulence, she gives us
blue skies, azure waters, brilliantly colored flowers, birds, and
other creations, with infinite variations* (p. 36).

THE still life before you has been arranged with much thought given to the
color and space relationships.   Use either oil paint or tempera.   Let us be as
little children.   Nothing to worry about—just self-expression.   What a joy!

First, we think of space.   Space is important because we live in it.   We
breathe in it.   All ratios, proportion, and action are in space.   Space is one and
we never go off base if we remember this.   It is infinite in width, infinite in
height, infinite in depth—there is no starting point or ending—it just is.   It is
more important to feel these things than to say them.   This gives us a joyous
sense of freedom which mentally means we can go anywhere.

In our painting, space becomes color and color becomes space.   Today,
we will particularly think of the power that color has to make us feel light.   We
will think of light as color and color as light.   Think of light as clarity and
order.   All these thoughts free us to become conscious of light moving in
space as color.   We cannot see forms in the dark.   We need light.   Man
cannot create light, but he can project the life of light by way of color.   We are
interested in pure color acting as light.   We are not bound to the color of the
objects, but we will feel free to use the color that expresses the flow of the
movement.   Since we must use our understanding to paint the space which

84

is not seen, it is logical that we should use a similar understanding to paint the objects which can be seen.

Spacial order, continuity of movement, movement of light, lead to that which is more profound than the material representation—lead to that which we call abstract qualities. There can be a deeper reality of the subject matter that has evolved abstractly than of the subject matter that has evolved from the appearance.

TREES

We set the mood by the first few things that happen. We cannot see the leaves actually growing, but we see the full blossom as evidence of the continuity of growth. And so it is with our progress (p. 30).

W E enjoy the expanse of a great horizontal like the spread of a great meadow. We enjoy the uprightness of trees. Feel as though you are in a magnificent forest. The great trees rise in the sky, shafts of glorious light pour through the space between the trees, shedding warmth and color upon the horizontal of the earth. The peace of a supernal beauty descends upon us. The glorious verticals of the trees are deeply rooted in the horizontal earth. We feel we are lending ourselves to the drama of great forces in nature. We might say that the principle of the sun is to nourish and glorify with the warmth of its inexpressible light. We might say that the principle of the earth is support and comfort. Let us express the superb drama of these three principles in our drawing and painting today.

Cezanne felt the essence of trees, of form, of nature. He was not conscious of style, but his deep desire to express to the utmost what he was feeling brought about his very own individual style. Great art transcends technique. The life forces, the love force is what projects—not physical aspects. Each one of us has the gift of individuality and, therefore, each one of us has an individual style.

APPROACH XXIX

FIGURE RELATED TO STILL LIFE

Caring for beauty and for mankind is the motive power for the art expression. It is a sharing. Profound music, poetry, and art inspire us with compassion, joy, and love (p. 17).

TODAY, we will work from the model and will combine this with a still life. Our model is sitting next to the still life, all uniting in one composition. Let us feel the contrasts of the relationships—the figure to the still life, the still life to the figure. The still life is on a small table of desk height. The head is upright above the still life. Let us spend time looking, absorbing the contents of the relationships. The space drops upon all and supports all.

The horizontal of the table with its still life unites and contrasts with the upright torso of the seated figure. Feel the largeness of the figure in contrast to the small elements of the still life. Study the elements of the still life in relationship to the figure and vice versa. Feel how one enhances the other until you feel the beauty of the flow of the one great composition.

The one composition includes the individuality of the still life, uniting with the individuality of the figure, forming a united composite individuality. Relying on the totality of the space, all will rhythmically fall into place.

87

APPROACH XXX

INTRODUCING BLACK
AS A COLOR

Self-discovery is a discovery of your own feeling. All true experience is a revelation of the self. That self includes the feeling for color (p. 38).

TODAY, choose three colors, one of which is black. Spend time choosing the other two colors. We are learning to use black as a positive color. The black color will acquire a living relationship in equality to the other colors instead of being used decoratively. This obliterates the tendency to avoid black or to use it for decorative embellishment.

We will apply our colors in rectangular areas touching one another. As in former approaches, we aim to feel that each area is related to the total. Feel that your choice of the color areas is motivated by feeling it deep in space and at the same time on the one great surface.

This approach helps us to sense the achievement of depth of space through color. It specifically helps us to use black in an authentic, magnificent way. Do not worry too much about the one great plane, for by placing the area in relationship to the total it will, of itself, be on the one plane.

All great art expression is involved with the control that gives the freedom. You are not leaning on the teacher, but on the guidance and the thinking that helps you to feel your own strength.

UTILIZING THE WORLD AROUND YOU

The artist has a direct path. Beethoven sustains us with the reality of glory or we could not soar with him. If we share the great depth of his experience we can soar (p. 24).

FOR our subject matter today, we will use what we see around us. We will take time to feel that every object or relationship we gaze upon is enveloped in living, paintable space. We will concentrate on forms and dynamics rather than on representation. The more conscious we become of the various forms ascending, descending, uniting, moving, the more we feel a bursting vitality. The vitality settles into equilibrium, the expansiveness into all-inclusiveness.

A doorway, a corner of a room, a floor, a window, everything our gaze rests upon can become entrancingly interesting. The more we feel the living reality of space, the more palatable everything becomes.

Art is not an escape. It is an act of truthfulness and liberation. A work of art gives one a feeling of reality which has a vitality of organization and of lasting quality.

The physical vision is involved with the appearance of temporal objects or scenes. The artist is involved with the eternal essence of objects and scenes and not with the temporal.

APPROACH XXXII

GREAT MOVEMENTS
LARGE MASSES

*Recognize when you are harmonious.   You are then ready for your
art work.   You are in tune, embraced in the beauty of infinite space.
The vast sense of what exists in the universe flows into the movement
of the painting* (p. 25).

LET us look at that which is around us.   We will translate that which is in
our immediate vision—great movements and large masses.

The camera eye might be seeing windows, doors, furniture, people, but
we are seeing forms with space.   We will translate what we see into painted
abstract forms that are living in painted space.

We begin to feel an underlying core of strength manifesting itself in great
movements.   Be patient and allow yourself the time to feel the large masses of
space and the large masses of form uniting in the rhythm of movement.   In this
particular approach, the space masses and the form masses should remain very
distinct, uniting but not merging.   You begin to feel them giving depth to
the total space.

Always your work must be meaningful to you.   Your sense of vision is
being developed as you practice this approach.

Matisse said that it was of the greatest importance to replace our automatic
physical vision with a newborn fresh vision.

90

There is no end to the revelation that comes from a highly developed vision. A crumpled piece of paper on the floor can become hills and valleys. A hanging drapery can seem like the streams of a waterfall. The verticals, the horizontals, the forms become alive with relationships. More and more we find infinite possibilities of our own development. Your own capacities are a constant revelation.

STARS — SPACE IS ALIVE
INFINITY

Individuality must be cherished and respected in oneself and in others. There is nothing as wonderful as the individual in that he has his own niche in eternity and no one can replace him (p. 21).

CHARCOAL. Even though we are in a class-room or a studio, we are going to enter the infinite world of a starry night. When we look up into the sky, we have a sense of infinite space. It seems to free and expand our vision. In the early evening, you have seen how a star suddenly seems to appear in the sky. That is the star you will draw. You will draw this as a small spherical mass, not as outline. Suddenly, you will see another star still deeper in space. Even though deeper in space, it will appear as a small spherical mass, the same size as the one before. Suddenly, still deeper in space, another star has appeared. After drawing that, again take time to feel another star still deeper in space than the others. Since space is infinite in depth, immeasurable, we can go on allowing another star and another star to appear deeper and deeper in the heavens. This must be done patiently and with the feeling that allows it to happen. Otherwise, the approach does not accomplish its purpose. Its purpose is to exercise your capacity to feel greater and greater depth in space. At the same time you will see how the surrounding areas of space are responding to your increasing number of stars. You will see that the white of the paper is beginning to move, that it seems to move on different levels. Animating the space by feeling greater and greater depth in the space is causing the aliveness of the space to be revealed, thus animating the whole composition.

We are feeling the glory of space. Our paper is revealing an infinity of space. Space, being alive,—it has no vacuums and no static area. Whatever we put into space reflects this aliveness and reveals the responding aliveness of the total space. Allow yourself to enter more and more deeply.

Art, being the reflection of life, is a force which is the reverse of the static. Art is dynamic and is never sustained within a finite static pattern. True art reflects the life-sustaining activity of the infinite universe. Its beauty is the reflection of the wondrous beauty of the living universe. The artist is sustained by using his native gift of intuition.

THE END